MW01103886

A 31-Day Experiment

Knowing God's Heart,
Sharing His Joy

OTHER BOOKS BY DICK PURNELL

A 31-DAY EXPERIMENT

REVISED & EXPANDED

Knowing GOD'S HEART, Sharing His Joy

DICK PURNELL

Publishers Since 1798

THOMAS NELSON PUBLISHERS

Nashville

Published in Nashville, Tennessee, by Thomas Nelson, Inc., Publishers, and distributed in Canada by Word Communications, Ltd., Richmond, British Columbia, and in the United Kingdom by Word (UK), Ltd., Milton Keynes, England.

Scripture quotations are taken from the HOLY BIBLE, NEW INTERNATIONAL VERSION ®. Copyright © 1973, 1978, 1984 by International Bible Society. Used by permission of Zondervan Bible Publishing House. All rights reserved.

The "NIV" and "New International Version" trademarks are registered in the United States Patent and Trademark Office by International Bible Society. Use of either trademark requires the permission of International Bible Society.

Library of Congress Cataloging-in-Publication Data

Purnell, Dick.
    Knowing God's heart, sharing his joy : a 31-day experiment / Dick Purnell. —Rev. & expanded.
        p.   cm.
    Originally published: San Bernardino, CA: Here's Life Publishers, 1988.
    Includes bibliographical references.
    ISBN 0-8407-6951-2 (pbk.)
    1. God—Worship and love. 2. God—Knowableness. 3. Devotional exercises. I. Title.
BV4817.P87 1993
248.3—dc20   92-44463
                                                         CIP

Printed in the United States of America
1 2 3 4 5 6 7 - 99 98 97 96 95 94 93

CONTENTS

DEDICATION

To my Single Life Resources team

Each of you has inspired me continually with your love for God and your enthusiastic commitment to spreading His life-changing message to needy people.

Our hearts beat as one with our dedication to telling people about God's desires for them.

ACKNOWLEDGMENTS

The ideas for this book came out of a meeting I had with five men. Each one was convinced of the need for a book that would motivate the reader—from the Scriptures—to communicate the gospel message with love and accuracy.

We spent hours praying and discussing key biblical teachings concerning salvation, evangelism, and God's desires for people. Most of the passages you will study in this Experiment were chosen as a result of that effort.

To these godly and loving men I give my deepest thanks:

Carl Broggi

Rick Hove

Richard Price

Terry Spinelli

Pat Springle

In addition to the above, Steve Douglass and Mark McCloskey gave me helpful advice in editing and refining, and I thank them.

GOD'S DESIRE FOR ALL PEOPLE

What causes you to do something for someone else?

Take this simple test. Place a check by each statement that reflects your motivation.

- ✓ You deeply love and appreciate him/her.
- It is a command from someone important.
- ✓ You know it is the right thing to do.
- ✓ That individual will be helped.
- ✓ You realize you also will benefit.
- ✓ Others have set an example for you to follow.

You probably have chosen the answers that reflect an "I want to" attitude, rather than an "I have to" obligation.

Here is another test.

What would motivate you to tell a person

about Christ and His message of salvation?

- You deeply love and appreciate him/her.
- God commanded you.
- You know it is the right thing to do.
- That individual will be helped.
- You realize you also will benefit.
- Others have set an example for you to follow.

All of these reasons are excellent, and each one can be found in the Bible. Yet it often seems so difficult for us to tell someone about our faith in the Lord. Why? The answer may be seen in a statement Christ made in Luke 6:45: "For out of the overflow of [a person's] heart his mouth speaks."

What fills your heart? What subjects fill your conversations?

Your heart represents the innermost center of your being. It is the source of your personality and emotions. What is in your heart will be on your lips and will determine your actions.

"I am trying to know God's heart."

Have you ever heard anyone say that? I haven't.

Of course, God does not have a physical heart. The term is only a figure of speech referring to His divine and eternal purposes. It would be wonderful to know the Lord's specific intentions for people, including yourself, wouldn't it?

If God were to allow you to enter the glory of His presence and inform you of His desire for all human beings, what would you do with that information? Your heart probably would burst with the news.

Here is something to get excited about. God actually is looking for people to know His heart. He promised to give leaders to ancient Israel—leaders who would represent His love and commitment to the people.

"I will give you shepherds after my own heart, who will lead you with knowledge and understanding" (Jeremiah 3:15). The Lord is searching for such people today.

Over a thousand years after King David of Israel lived, the apostle Paul said this about him:

"[God] made David their King. He testified concerning him: 'I have found David son of Jesse a man after my own heart; he will do everything I want him to do.' From this man's descendants God has brought to Israel the Savior Jesus, as he promised." (Acts 13:22–23)

What a stunning tribute! The Lord wanted you and me to know the inner motivations of a man who lived three thousand years ago and what God accomplished through his influence. Would you like Christ to say the same thing about you? He can if you will do the same things to please Him that David did.

SET YOUR HEART ON GOD'S HEART

In the depths of his being, David sought to know God and the complexity of His character. It wasn't just a passing fad for him. It was his life's ambition. This Experiment will help you saturate your mind and soul with God's heart. Ask Him to show you what He sees and to fill you with what He feels.

When [Jesus] saw the crowds, he had compassion on them, because they were harassed and helpless, like sheep without a shepherd. Then he said to his disciples, "The harvest is plentiful but the workers are few. Ask the Lord of the harvest, therefore, to send out workers into his harvest field." (Matthew 9:36–38)

FOLLOW HIS DIRECTIONS WHOLE-HEARTEDLY

King Saul, who preceded David on the throne of Israel, obeyed God only half-heartedly (1 Samuel 15:1–35). King Solomon, David's son who succeeded him, allowed his heart to be turned away from the Lord (1 Kings 11:1–6). God punished both of them.

David was different. Obedience to God's will was his passion. Yes, he did sin greatly. But he returned to the Lord with all his energy. God said of him, "My servant David . . . kept my commands and followed me with all his heart, doing only what was right in my eyes" (1 Kings 14:8).

Love and obedience go together. Christ said, "Whoever has my commands and obeys them, he is the one who loves me. He who loves me will be loved by my Father, and I too will love him and show myself to him" (John 14:21).

The privilege of closeness with God comes as a result of observing the responsibility of doing His will. As you study the Scriptures this month, respond with love and obedience to the information the Lord gives you.

A joyful, godly life is one of the most attractive incentives there is for a person to come to Christ. He wants you to have that.

DETERMINE TO LEAVE A GODLY LEGACY

God honored David by bringing the Savior into the world through his family tree. His faithfulness left a powerful witness of godliness and joyful worship. What will your spiritual family tree look like?

God's heart will fill you with joy and with the courage to share His message of salvation with people who walk in darkness. Only two things will last forever: the Word of God and the souls of people. The more you fill your heart with the purposes of God, the more you will spontaneously and enthusiastically fill your speech with His goodness. And many of those who hear will follow your example and put their faith in Christ.

TRY THIS EXPERIMENT

This book is designed to give you the biblical motivation for evangelism (sharing the gospel of salvation with other people). It is not a book of methods. When you understand God's perspective and purpose for all people, you will want to learn to communicate His heart with others more effectively.

For the next 31 days let God draw you into His confidence. As you work through this Experiment, the Scriptures will come alive with the heartbeat of our Heavenly Father. Have a heart-to-heart talk with Him each day. You will be amazed at the incredibly wonderful things you will learn.

Seek continually to know God's heart more deeply. Your own heart will be full, and you will experience the thrill of bringing others into the same kind of loving relationship with the Lord.

MY PRAYER

Dear Compassionate Lord,

Your love and Your kindness toward me is overwhelming. Because of my self-centeredness and my disobedience I was headed straight toward eternal damnation and hell.

But You brought Your message of forgiveness and eternal life to me. You saved me from destruction and hopelessness.

Thank You for the way You reached me and for the people who helped me turn humbly to You. I will be forever grateful for their witness to me, and for my salvation.

Even with all You have done for me, I am often too busy or too afraid to share my faith with others. Sometimes, I don't even care.

Change me! Inspire my heart with Your heart. As I spend the next 31 days doing this Experiment, saturate my mind with Your thoughts. Inflame my soul with a passion to encourage others to follow You.

I want to experience the Holy Spirit's power

working through me to bring others to know You. O King of Kings, thank You for making me Your ambassador to bring Your message of love and forgiveness to a needy world.

I love You with my whole heart.

In Your wonderful name I pray.

Signed _____

MY COVENANT WITH GOD

I commit myself before God to do this Experiment for the next 31 days. Today, I make a covenant with the Lord Jesus to:

1. Spend up to 30 minutes each day in Bible study, prayer, and writing out my thoughts and plans.

2. Ask at least one other Christian to pray daily for me that the Experiment will help me grow in faith (that person may want to do the Experiment along with me so we can share together what we are learning).

3. Attend a church each week where the Word of God is taught and I am encouraged to share my faith with others.

Signed _Bottie Waugh_

Date _10-2-97_

WHERE TO BEGIN

A. PREPARATION FOR EACH DAY

1. *Equipment.* Have a Bible and pen to record your thoughts and plans in this book.
2. *Time.* Choose a specific half-hour each day to spend with the Lord. Pick the time of day that is best for you—when your heart is most receptive to meeting with God.
3. *Place.* Find a particular spot where you can clear your mind of distractions and focus your full attention on God's Word. Suggestions: bedroom, office, library, living room, lounge, outdoors.

B. READ—20 Minutes

1. Pray earnestly before you begin. Ask the Lord to teach you what He desires you to learn.
2. Read the entire passage.

3. Read it again, looking for important ideas.
4. Make written notes on the following:
   a. Sections A and B—Study the passage thoroughly to answer the questions. Focus your attention on the attributes and actions of our Lord. The more you know about Him, the more you will be able to trust Him to work in and through your life.
   b. Section C—Write out your personal responses and specifically apply to your life the lessons you have learned.
5. Choose a verse that is especially meaningful to you. Copy it onto a card and read it several times during the day. Think about its meaning and impact on your life. Memorize it when you have free mental time, for example, when you are getting ready in the morning, while you are standing in line, taking a coffee break, waiting for class to begin, or walking somewhere.

C. NEED—5 Minutes
   1. Choose what is your most pressing per-

sonal need of the day.

2. Write down your request. The more specific you are, the more specific the answer will be.

3. Earnestly pray each day for the provision of the Sovereign Lord. Trust Him for big things.

4. When the Heavenly Father meets your need, record the date and how He did it. Periodically review the Good Shepherd's wonderful provisions, and thank Him often for His faithfulness. This will greatly increase your faith.

5. At the end of the month, review all the answers to your prayers. Rejoice in God's goodness to you. Keep praying for the requests that still need answers.

D. DEED—5 Minutes

1. Pray for God's guidance to help another person during the day. Try to apply the particular passage you have just studied.

2. Take the initiative to express God's wonderful love to someone. Be a servant. Someone has said, "Behind every face there is a drama going on." Tap into

at least one person's drama.

3. As you help a needy person, tell him (or her) about your faith in Christ. Here are some suggestions for helping:
   a. Provide a meal.
   b. Take care of his/her children.
   c. Help him/her study for a school subject.
   d. Do yard work.
   e. Write an encouraging letter.
   f. Start a Bible study.
   g. Teach a sports activity or a mechanical skill.
   h. Fix something.
   i. Show interest in his/her interests.
   j. Give an honest compliment.
   k. Pray with him about his/her need.

4. Later, record the details of how the Holy Spirit used you this day. This will increase your confidence to reach out to others. Thank the Lord Jesus for expressing His love and compassion to others through you.

E. APPLICATION

1. Write down ideas about how you would put into practice specific lessons found

in the passage.
2. Devise a plan to implement your ideas.

F. LAST THING IN THE EVENING
1. READ the passage again, looking for additional about God and about His desire for people to know Him.
2. Pray again for your **NEED**. Thank the Lord that He will answer in His way and in His time. Expect the Spirit of the Living God to strengthen you in your walk with Him.
3. Record the **DEED** God guided you to accomplish.
4. Review the **APPLICATION** you chose for the day.

G. PARTNERS
Ask a friend or a group of friends to do the Experiment together with you. Pray frequently for one another that you will learn more about the Lord and how to lovingly communicate His message to others. Encourage one another to be disciplined and faithful in completing the Experiment. Share what you are learning.

THE EXPERIMENT

31 Days

of

Knowing
God's Heart,
Sharing His Joy

Section 1

Knowing God's Heart

Days 1–12

SOMETHING TO GET EXCITED ABOUT

Psalm 67:1–7

▼

KEY VERSES:
May God be gracious to us and bless us and make his face shine upon us, that your ways may be known on earth, your salvation among all nations (Psalm 67:1–2).

TODAY'S FOCUS:
The good news of God's wonderful offer of salvation is worth getting excited about. As the psalmist says, "Be glad and sing for joy!"

READ:
Pray for a heart of praise.

DAY 1

A. What does God want all nations and peoples to know?

Salvation

B. What should everyone do?

Praise God

C. Here are things I praise God for:

a warm home
a single unified mind
means to be hospitable
great friends

DAY 1

NEED:

Pray for God's face to shine on you.

My greatest need today is: money to pay the bills on time; money for trip to az.

God has been gracious to me by answering my prayer on _10-10_ (date). Here is how He did it: more work on the boats; my boss giving me my paycheck before I leave.

DEED:

Pray for your nation to know God's salvation.

O God, lead me to someone who needs: Encouragement to come to church- Like Debbie from TW; Denise;

▲

APPLICATION:

Continue praising God for His heart for the world by joyfully responding to Psalm 98.

SINGING A NEW SONG

Psalm 96:1–13

▼

KEY VERSES:
Sing to the LORD a new song; sing to the LORD,
all the earth. Sing to the LORD, praise his name;
proclaim his salvation day after day (Psalm
96:1–2).

TODAY'S FOCUS:
The Lord is great and most worthy of praise!
Even nature can't help but proclaim the mighty
works of God.

READ:
Pray for joy.

A. What are we to tell the nations?

about the Glory of God.

B. Why should all of the earth worship the Lord? He created it.

C. This is what I will sing to Him:

Your mountain tops are grand, your ocean floors like treasure, the birds fill our ♥'s c̄ song, the flowers our eyes c̄ beauty our noses c̄ fragrance, all nature speaks of you?

29

DAY 2

NEED:

Thank the Lord for His marvelous deeds.

My greatest need today is: _Spiritual discernment, a heart of understanding towards Corrine - that I may transfer my heart for God to her heart in need._

Today __10-4__ (date) the Lord was faithful to His promises. He met my need in this way:

I knew what she needed to hear to help her get closer to you.

DEED:

Pray for enthusiasm to proclaim good tidings.

I want others to know that: _Nature itself speaks of God!_

▲

APPLICATION:

Compose a song, poem, or letter to God that expresses your reaction to His greatness.

(see note bk)

A PURPOSE FOR LIVING

Isaiah 42:1–9

▼

KEY VERSES:
I will keep you and will make you to be a covenant for the people and a light for the Gentiles, to open eyes that are blind, to free captives from prison and to release from the dungeon those who sit in darkness (Isaiah 42:6–7).

TODAY'S FOCUS:
Christ came to fulfill this law of God. As His followers, we have the same call of God. This is our purpose for living, our compelling aspiration.

READ:
Pray that you will accept God's call.

DAY 3

A. Jesus Christ, God's servant, had a purpose in coming to the nations. How would He act?

In faithfullness he will bring justice.

B. What did God appoint Him to do?

be a covenant for the people, a light shining in the darkness

C. As a servant of Christ, I want to follow His lead to:

let my light shine, allow my faithfulness to speak greatly of God -

DAY 3

NEED:

Thank God for taking hold of your hand.

My greatest need today is: *Put myself aside, while not ignoring my physical needs.*

God the Lord responded to my plea today _____ (date) by:

DEED:

Pray that God will use you to help open blind spiritual eyes.

Lord God, hold me by the hand and do this through me:

▲

APPLICATION:

In one to two sentences write out your purpose in life. Why are you on this earth? What are you living for? *To seek + save the lost, to help others to know God + the freedom that comes from being forgiven.*

WHEN HEAVEN REJOICES

Luke 15:1–10

▼

KEY VERSE:
"In the same way, I tell you, there is rejoicing in the presence of the angels of God over one sinner who repents" (Luke 15:10).

TODAY'S FOCUS:
God deeply cares for the lost. The heavenly beings rejoice more when one sinner repents than over ninety-nine righteous people who don't need to repent! That's something to think about.

READ:
Pray that the lost will be found.

DAY 4

A. Christ used this parable (illustration) to describe God's search for sinners to bring them back to Himself. Describe His desires:

To have the lost back in his arms.

B. What are the responses in heaven when a sinner repents (confesses his sin and humbly turns to follow God)? Why?

Rejoicing - the person will soon be a part of heaven.

C. Like the man pursuing one sheep and the woman searching for one coin, I am determined to:

Bring Debbie + Jim into the fold

DAY 4

NEED:
Pray for determination to search for the lost.
My greatest need today is:

Humble heart when discipled.

The God of compassion helped me on _____
(date) in this manner:

DEED:
Pray that sinners will repent.
Good Shepherd, strengthen and direct me to:

Be a great example at work of a gentle non-judgmental person.

APPLICATION:
Continue reading Luke 15 to understand what happens to the lost son. List the characteristics of the father. He is a picture of God the Father.

TESTIMONY OF A TAX COLLECTOR

Luke 19:1–10

▼

KEY VERSE:
For the Son of Man came to seek and to save what was lost (Luke 19:10).

TODAY'S FOCUS:
Despite public criticism, Jesus boldly and compassionately reached out to the social outcasts around Him—those who needed Him most. He had a mission to accomplish.

READ:
Pray that your heart will reflect Jesus' heart for people.

A. How did Zacchaeus respond to Jesus? Why did Jesus go to him?

Joyful, faith-filled -

J. saw his faith

B. Jesus changed the life of another tax collector. In Mark 2:13–17 how did Levi (Matthew) respond to Jesus? Why did Jesus go to him?

Had him over to dinner

J. knew he was lost +

needed salvation

C. This is why I will seek sinners:

They are lost + need to see

God.

DAY 5

NEED:

Pray for lost loved ones.
My greatest need today is:

Humility in being discipled.

Today _____ (date) the Son of Man answered
my prayer in this way:

DEED:

Pray for opportunities to bring Jesus to the lost.
Son of Man, seek and save the lost through
me by: *Allowing me to show the
difference at work*

▲

APPLICATION:

Jesus sought out another social outcast. Read
about it in John 4:1–42. Why do you think He
went to these kinds of people?

*They had lost hope for life to
be better.*

LIFE WITHOUT GOD

Ecclesiastes 2:1–26

▼

KEY VERSE:
Yet when I surveyed all that my hands had done and what I had toiled to achieve, everything was meaningless, a chasing after the wind; nothing was gained under the sun (Ecclesiastes 2:11).

TODAY'S FOCUS:
Partying, achievements, possessions, success, popularity, riches—without God they come to nothing. Life apart from God is empty. Only He brings true and lasting satisfaction.

READ:
Pray for understanding of the meaning of your life.

DAY 6

A. King Solomon endeavored to find lasting fulfillment. What did he do to try to find happiness? *Built things, bought anything he desired, denied himself nothing.*

B. He concluded that everything was "chasing after the wind" (futile and empty) without God. What can only God do for a person? (See also Ecclesiastes 3:9–14.)

   Give wisdom + joy.

C. The source of my happiness is: *the Hope that I will go on to heaven when my life is over.*

41

NEED:

Pray for God's wisdom and knowledge.
   My greatest need today is:

Discipline in eating - not to give in to urges?

The hand of God has provided for me today
_____ (date) the following:

DEED:

Pray for people who are without God.
   Lord, only You can make life worthwhile. Use
   me to tell others that:

You are real + worth getting to know.

▲

APPLICATION:

List the things you have tried in order to find
meaning. What have you learned about the
meaning of life? Read Ecclesiastes 12:13–14 to
find out Solomon's conclusion.

Education, Possessions, Prowning in self absorbtion.

None else matters but knowing + fearing God.

WE ARE ALL IN THE SAME BOAT

Romans 3:9–31

▼

KEY VERSES:
For all have sinned and fall short of the glory of God, and are justified freely by his grace through the redemption that came by Christ Jesus (Romans 3:23–24).

TODAY'S FOCUS:
Every human chooses to be independent from God. We are all sinful. No one is perfect. God's offer of salvation is freely available to anyone and everyone.

READ:
Thank God for His righteousness.

DAY 7

A. As far as God is concerned, what is true of every person in the world?

They have sinned + fallen short of His glory

B. What does it mean to be justified before God? How does a person become justified?

Just as if I had not sinned

- through faith in J. Christ

C. I know I am justified because:

As a result of my faith I believed + chose to follow Jesus - was Baptized + now live a new life -

DAY 7

NEED:

Pray for increased confidence in God.

My greatest need today is:

Time to do all I need to get done.

Christ Jesus again showed me His love by answering my prayer today __10·10__ (date) in this way: *I can't believe all that I acomplished - laundry, sewing, I was super organized + found what I needed +*

DEED:

Pray for people who are still under sin. *decisive*

Lord Jesus, thank You for providing the basis *when* for justification by sacrificially dying on the *needed* cross. Lead me to people who: *to be*

▲

APPLICATION:

Look on page 130 in the section entitled, "Important Words to Understand." There you will find definitions of important biblical words, including several found in today's passage.

RESTORATION OF A BROKEN MAN

Psalm 51:1–17

▼

KEY VERSE:
Create in me a pure heart, O God, and renew a
steadfast spirit within me (Psalm 51:10).

TODAY'S FOCUS:
Sin is what separates you from God. The Lord
desires sin to be confessed to Him. When you
come before Him with a broken and contrite
heart, He is able to restore the joy of salvation.

READ:
Pray for a broken and contrite heart.

DAY 8

A. Sin is an attitude of independence from God and a transgression of His law. Why should a person seek to be cleansed of his iniquity (sin)?

That she may be restored to God's glory - and have eternal life c̄ Him.

B. What will God do for a person who humbly confesses his sin and turns from his evil ways?

wash away the guilt of the sin.

C. Having a "clean heart" means to me:

Confessing my attitudes and dealing openly with any emotions that separate me from others.

NEED:

Pray for truth in your innermost being.

My greatest need today is:

A heart of peace; a diligence to get things done.

The God of my salvation responded to my need on _____ (date) by:

DEED:

Pray for wisdom to teach transgressors God's ways.

Dear Lord, may sinners be converted to You through my witness. Help me to:

▲

APPLICATION:

David knew how unconfessed sin could adversely affect a person. Read his testimony in Psalm 32.

A HEAVENLY MESSAGE ABOUT TWO KINDS OF PEOPLE

John 3:1–21

▼

KEY VERSE:
For God so loved the world that he gave his one and only Son, that whoever believes in him shall not perish but have eternal life (John 3:16).

TODAY'S FOCUS:
Everyone must make a choice: to believe in Jesus Christ, resulting in eternal life, or to reject Christ, resulting in condemnation and separation from God.

READ:
Pray for discernment to seek out God's view of things.

A. Jesus witnessed to an important leader of Israel. Even though Nicodemus was a professional educator, he was missing the key to eternal life. What is it? How can you know for certain that you have eternal life?

Baptism —
I repented of my sins
when I believed +
was Baptized into
Jesus for the forgiveness
of those sin + have the gift of
the Holy Spirit

B. What are the characteristics of a believer? An unbeliever?

Follows Jesus, open + honest life -
brings others to Him;

Selfishly does as they choose, no
desire to draw others to their way
of life

C. I know I am born again because:

I was baptized as a disciple
on
March 7th 1990
at 10.30pm

DAY 9

NEED:

Pray for commitment to live by the truth.
My greatest need today is:

To reflect Jesus' life in all my encounters.

The Son of God gave His answer today _____
(date). Here is how He did it:

DEED:

Pray for a life consistent with your new birth.
O Lord, just as You witnessed, I want to do
the same. Bring someone to me who:

▲

APPLICATION:

Finish reading John 3. What did John believe
about Jesus?

He was the messiah prophisied about.

FROM DEATH TO LIFE

Ephesians 2:1–10

▼

KEY VERSES:

But because of his great love for us, God, who is rich in mercy, made us alive with Christ even when we were dead in transgressions—it is by grace you have been saved (Ephesians 2:4–5).

TODAY'S FOCUS:

God loves people so much that He provided a way from death to life—a way that cannot be earned, bought, or bargained for. It is a free gift, given to those who put their faith in Christ.

READ:

Thank God for His love for people.

A. Describe the condition of an individual living without Christ in his life (see also Ephesians 4:17-24):

Futile in thinking
Seeking worldly pleasure,
Sensitivity, Sexuality.

B. What changes does God produce in the person who puts his faith in Christ?

a pure heart + purpose

C. I put my faith in Christ because:

He is the way to heaven,
the truth that never fails
and a guiding beacon of light
in my life.

NEED:
Thank God you are His workmanship. Pray for Christ's resurrection power.

My greatest need today is:

God is rich in mercy and grace. On _____ (date) this is what He did for me:

DEED:
Pray to do good works.

Dear God, help me to walk in good works. Guide me to:

▲

APPLICATION:
The resurrection of Christ is the key to receiving new life. Read 1 Corinthians 15 to learn the importance of His rising from the dead.

BASIS OF OUR SALVATION

Titus 3:1–8

▼

KEY VERSES:
But when the kindness and love of God our
Savior appeared, he saved us, not because of
righteous things we had done, but because of his
mercy (Titus 3:4–5).

TODAY'S FOCUS:
Why did God save you? Not because of anything
you might have done, but because of His love,
kindness, and mercy. He cares about you that
much!

READ:
Thank God for His kindness and love.

DAY 11

A. What has God done for the believer?

Poured out grace + mercy
upon me.

B. Write down the definitions of the following
words (if you need help, look at the section
entitled "Important Words to Understand"
on page 130):

1. Salvation - To be forgiven of all my
   sins, to be reconciled to God
2. Mercy - God's love show by not keeping
   track of my sin
3. Renewal/Regeneration -

4. Justification - Jesus paid the penalty
   for me -
5. Grace - God's desire to forgive me
   of my sin.

C. I know Jesus is my Savior because:

I was baptized as a disciple
for my belief in him that
my sins are forgiven

DAY 11

NEED:
Thank God for eternal life.
My greatest need today is:

God's Holy Spirit answered my prayer on
_____ (date). This is how:

DEED:
Pray for opportunities to do good.
Dear God, I am trusting You to:

▲

APPLICATION:
For an in-depth study of what God has done for
us, examine Romans 5–6.

SUPERNATURAL LIFE FOR ORDINARY PEOPLE

2 Peter 1:1–12

▼

KEY VERSE:

His divine power has given us everything we need for life and godliness through our knowledge of him who called us by his own glory and goodness (2 Peter 1:3).

TODAY'S FOCUS:

Through His divine power, you are enabled to live the Christian life. The more you get to know Jesus Christ, the more effective and productive your life will be.

READ:

Thank God for His great and precious promises.

DAY 12

A. God has given fantastic things to all who have believed in Jesus Christ. What has He given to us? an awesome worldwide kingdom that no matter where I go I can be a part of.

B. How can we increase godly qualities in our daily lives? Read + Study the Bible + put it into practice.

C. With Christ's divine power, I am determined to: Help someone become a Christian before I get married.

DAY 12

NEED:

Pray for diligence to develop godly qualities.
My greatest need today is:

My Lord and Savior Jesus Christ abundantly
supplied my needs today _____ (date) in
this way:

DEED:

Pray that you will become useful and fruitful for
Christ.
I am your bond-servant to:

Serve Debbie in every way —
to show Christs love through
everything.

APPLICATION:

The quality of life God has for His own people is
far superior to anything the world offers. Read
Colossians 3:1–25 and Romans 12:1–21 to learn
about other qualities to develop.

THE EXPERIMENT

31 Days

of

Knowing God's Heart, Sharing His Joy

Section 2

Sharing His Joy

Days 13–31

GOD'S DESIRE FOR ALL NATIONS

Matthew 28:1–20

▼

KEY VERSES:

Therefore go and make disciples of all nations, baptizing them in the name of the Father and of the Son and of the Holy Spirit, and teaching them to obey everything I have commanded you. And surely I am with you always, to the very end of the age (Matthew 28:19–20).

TODAY'S FOCUS:

If you have met the risen Christ, the most wonderful thing you can do for someone else is share your discovery and joy. Sharing the good news with "all nations" begins one person at a time.

READ:

Pray for joyful obedience.

DAY 13

A. Why did the women and the disciples worship Jesus?

He had risen from the dead.

B. What does the risen Christ command you to do in all nations?

make disciples

C. Because the Lord Jesus has all authority in heaven and on earth, I will:

Obey + make disciples of all nations.

NEED:

Thank the Lord that He is always with you!

My greatest need today is: To be there for Deb & energy - to serve whole heartedly.

The risen Christ met my need today
_____ (date) in this way:

DEED:

Pray for a lifestyle of making disciples.

Thank you, Lord, that You are always with me. Therefore, I ask You to:

▲

APPLICATION:

This passage is called "The Great Commission."
Read the other commissions that Jesus gave in
Mark 16:14–16, Luke 24:44–49, John 20:19–23,
and Acts 1:1–8.

THE DIVINE ENERGIZER

Acts 1:1–11

▼

KEY VERSE:
But you will receive power when the Holy Spirit
comes on you; and you will be my witnesses in
Jerusalem, and in all Judea and Samaria, and
to the ends of the earth (Acts 1:8).

TODAY'S FOCUS:
Jesus promised His disciples that He would
send the Holy Spirit, and they would receive
power to witness. That same power is available
to you!

READ:
Pray for God's supernatural power.

A. The Lord Jesus commanded us to tell people everywhere about Him. How can we carry out this awesome responsibility?

The discipling ministry -
I create one disciple, we
Create 2 disciples, and so on -
planting churches worldwide.

B. A believer is baptized by the Holy Spirit into the Body of Christ at the moment of salvation (1 Corinthians 12:13). Because He is *in* you, what else will the Holy Spirit do *for* you (read Romans 8:5–11)?

Give power + life to
my body

C. I believe that the Spirit of God is in me because: I was baptized for
the forgiveness of my sin
after I heard the truth +
believed.

DAY 14

NEED:
Thank God that the Holy Spirit lives in you.
My greatest need today is:

A humble, joy-filled heart during work + D-time after.

The Holy Spirit is wonderful. Today _____
(date) He:

DEED:
Pray for the Holy Spirit to empower you to
witness.
Oh Lord, I want to be a faithful messenger.
Help me to: *Stand out at work as a joy, not a complainer. Let a true light shine in my Christianity.* ▲

APPLICATION:
The Holy Spirit is our source of supernatural
power to live the Christian life as God desires
us to do. Read John 16:7–14 to understand His
working in you and in the world.

SEIZING THE OPPORTUNITY

Acts 3:11–26

▼

KEY VERSE:
Repent, then, and turn to God, so that your sins
may be wiped out, that times of refreshing may
come from the Lord (Acts 3:19).

TODAY'S FOCUS:
Every day you are given opportunities to share
with others who Jesus is and what He has done.
You just need to take advantage of them!

READ:
Pray that God will use you mightily in
someone's life.

A. Peter responded to a needy lame man by healing him (Acts 3:1–10). This sparked amazement and curiosity in the people—they wanted to know what had happened. So Peter enthusiastically witnessed to them. Why did they need to repent?

They were in sin + didn't believe what was said + done about Jesus.

B. What would God do when they put their faith in Jesus?

allow times of Refreshing to come.

C. I desire for people to know that:

I have overcome drug addiction, eating disorders, and MPD only because of God.

NEED:

Pray for times of refreshing to come from the Lord.

My greatest need today is:

Jesus, the Holy and Righteous One, has blessed me today _____ (date) by:

DEED:

Pray for opportunities to tell others about Jesus.

Dear Prince of Life, open the minds of people to become curious about You so that I may:

Share how you have been there for me through it all!

▲

APPLICATION:

Peter's confident boldness led to interesting events. Read about them in Acts 4.

WHO ARE YOU GOING TO OBEY?

Acts 5:17–42

▼

KEY VERSE:
Peter and the other apostles replied: "We must obey God rather than men!" (Acts 5:29)

TODAY'S FOCUS:
In the face of opposition, we can boldly and confidently proclaim our steadfast commitment to the Lord. We take orders from our Prince and Savior, Jesus Christ.

READ:
Pray for determination.

A. Peter and the other apostles (the men uniquely chosen by Christ) couldn't be stopped by opposition or hostility. What caused them to continue to witness?

> The heartfelt conviction that
> all others were lost +
> needed salvation.

B. What makes the message of Christ attractive to some people? What makes it unattractive to others?

> Unconditional love freely given
> attracts some.
> Others don't want to submit

C. I will follow Peter's example in this way:

> To preach/ share regardless of
> shame that may be brought.

DAY 16

NEED:
Pray that you will obey God rather than men.
My greatest need today is:

I know God is powerful. He has met my need today _____ (date) by:

DEED:
Pray for boldness to teach others about Christ.
Holy Spirit, fill me with Your power to:

▲

APPLICATION:
The Holy Spirit gives the power to live for Christ and to speak His message. Read Acts 2 to find out what happened when He empowered the disciples.

THE REALITY OF THE RESURRECTION

Acts 17:16–34

▼

KEY VERSES:
God did this so that men would seek him and perhaps reach out for him and find him, though he is not far from each one of us. "For in him we live and move and have our being" (Acts 17:27–28).

TODAY'S FOCUS:
The central theme of the good news of Jesus Christ is the fact of His death and resurrection. This joyful truth is the foundation for the uniqueness of the gospel as opposed to all other religions.

READ:
Pray for power to teach God's truth.

A. Paul took the initiative to talk boldly about Christ and to reason with curious people. What did He want them to know about God?

God was and is our creator —
and Jesus who he raised
from the dead will judge all
people — believers or not.

B. Why is the resurrection of Jesus key to the message of the gospel?

It is the only way to be
Saved — God cannot have
the imperfect with Him.

C. Regardless of the responses of people to the gospel, I will:

Continue to live a life
of faith, continue to
share that faith c̄ others.

DAY 17

NEED:
Pray for sensitivity to the needs of others.
My greatest need today is:

The risen Christ answered my prayer today
____(date) in this way:

DEED:
Pray for understanding to know how to reason
with unbelievers.
Dear God, make Yourself known to others
through me by:

See a difference in how I put
my christianity into practice.

▲

APPLICATION:
Christianity is unique among all religions be-
cause it is based on the resurrection of its leader.
Read John 20 to understand its importance.

DISOBEDIENCE BRINGS PAIN

Jonah 1:1–2:10

▼

KEY VERSE:
But I, with a song of thanksgiving, will sacrifice to you. What I have vowed I will make good. Salvation comes from the LORD (Jonah 2:9).

TODAY'S FOCUS:
Disobedience to God's commands results in negative consequences—it always has and it always will. Fortunately, God is gracious. Repentance and obedience bring forgiveness and reconciliation.

READ:
Pray that you will learn from Jonah's experience.

DAY 18

A. God told Jonah to give His message to Nineveh, the capital of the barbaric Assyrians who fiercely ruled the known world. What was Jonah's response? What were the consequences?

No; he ran from the Lord, but he didn't escape Him.

B. Why did God release Jonah from the great fish?

His heart had changed — now he could carry out God's command.

C. It is important to give God's message to needy people because:

It is there way of seeing the salvation of God — the way out God has for them

NEED:
Thank the Lord for your salvation.
  My greatest need today is:

  The Lord God of heaven heard my cry and
  answered today _____ (date) in this manner:

DEED:
Pray for obedience to God's commands.
  O Lord my God, rescue me from my fears and
  hesitancy. Give me a responsive heart to:

▲

APPLICATION:
What happened to Jonah and Nineveh? Read
Jonah 3 and 4 to see the conclusion of this
fascinating event.

RESPONSES THAT REVEAL THE HEART

Luke 8:4–15

▼

KEY VERSE:
But the seed on good soil stands for those with a noble and good heart, who hear the word, retain it, and by persevering produce a crop (Luke 8:15).

TODAY'S FOCUS:
When you sow the seed of God's Word in someone's life, the results are not up to you. It is God who prepares the soil and makes things grow. A person's reaction reveals his or her attitudes toward God.

READ:
Pray for ears that will hear Christ.

A. When you sow the seed of God's Word, people react in a variety of ways. List the different responses and the consequences they produce.

B. Christ spoke in parables so that His followers would understand. Unbelievers would miss the message because they refused to obey God's commands. What did Christ mean by "He who has ears to hear, let him hear" (verse 8)?

Anyone c̄ a heart open to the message would hear and understand.

C. Of the four types of soil, I am:

Good soil - persevering to produce a crop.

DAY 19

NEED:

Pray that you will bear fruit through perseverance.

My greatest need today is:

The Lord God heard and answered my prayer on _____ (date) in this way:

DEED:

Pray that you will sow lots of seed onto good soil.

Lord, I want to be a faithful source of God's Word. Lead me to people who will:

▲

APPLICATION:

This same parable is given in Matthew 13:1–23 and Mark 4:1–20. Compare the passages and consider the implications of the way people react to God's Word.

WAYS TO WIN PEOPLE

1 Corinthians 9:16–27

▼

KEY VERSE:
I have become all things to all men so that by all
possible means I might save some (1 Corinthians 9:22).

TODAY'S FOCUS:
Everyone is different. A willingness to meet
people where they are is vital to your witness.
Start with their interests and people will listen
to your interests.

READ:
Pray for flexibility in your approach.

A. What did Paul do to win people to Christ?

Became like them —
was relatable to many
people.

B. What motivated Paul to witness?

The salvation that he knew,
to spread to others.

C. Here are some things I plan to do in order
to bring more people to Christ:

Dinners with people,
Inviting to church whoever
I come in contact with.

NEED:
Pray to be a disciplined person.
  My greatest need today is:

  Thank You, Lord, that You answered my
  prayer today _____ (date) by:

DEED:
Pray for opportunities to share the gospel.
  Lord Jesus, I ask You to:

———▲———

APPLICATION:
Write down the names of three people with
whom you want to share about Christ. Indicate
their major interests and how you will present
the gospel using those areas.

TESTIMONY OF AN EVIL KING

2 Chronicles 33:1–20

▼

KEY VERSE:
And when he prayed to him, the LORD was moved by his entreaty and listened to his plea; so he brought him back to Jerusalem and to his kingdom. Then Manasseh knew that the LORD is God (2 Chronicles 33:13).

TODAY'S FOCUS:
No matter how evil a person is, God can still transform his or her life. No one is so "lost" that God cannot save that person if he or she becomes humble before Him.

READ:
Pray for people who seem uninterested in God.

A. Of all the kings of the nation of Judah, Manasseh was the most evil. What are some of the abominations he was involved in?

> Idol worship
> Sorcery, divination
> Offered his sons as
> sacrifice to other gods.

B. Why did God forgive him? What changes did the Lord bring about in Manasseh's life?

> His heart changed when
> he saw what God had
> done for him.

C. Reading about Manasseh has encouraged me to:

DAY 21

NEED:

Pray for God's transforming power.
My greatest need today is:

Almighty God revealed His power today
_____ (date) in answering my prayer by:

DEED:

Pray that unbelievers will humble themselves
greatly before God.

O Lord God, if You can forgive and change
Manasseh, You can do the same for:

▲

APPLICATION:

Describe how God has changed you. What difference has He made in your life? Share your testimony with someone today.

PEOPLE WHO ARE POSSESSED BY GOD

Titus 2:1–14

▼

KEY VERSES:

We wait for the blessed hope—the glorious appearing of our great God and Savior, Jesus Christ, who gave himself for us to redeem us from all wickedness and to purify for himself a people that are his very own, eager to do what is good (Titus 2:13–14).

TODAY'S FOCUS:

Your life is a testimony. Your attitudes, actions, words, and deeds in everyday situations speak volumes to the non-Christian world about your faith in Christ

READ:

Thank God for His grace and salvation.

DAY 22

A. Describe the characteristics you believe God wants you to develop in your life.

Gentle spirit, hard worker at home, self-controlled.

B. Why does the Lord want you to live in this manner?

To be an example of devotion — to God, my (future) husband, to be an example to all I am in contact with.

C. My God and Savior, make me the kind of person who:

Works diligently without complain

NEED:

Pray that you will live a self-controlled, upright, and godly life.

My greatest need today is:

How I thank Christ Jesus today _____ (date) for:

DEED:

Pray to be eager to do what is good.

Dear Savior, thank You for redeeming me. Use me to bring Your salvation to:

———▲———

APPLICATION:

To consistently display the kind of life that honors God and attracts unbelievers to Christ, you need to understand the source of life described in John 15:1–8. What does it mean to "remain in Christ"?

WOLVES IN CHRISTIAN CLOTHING

1 John 2:18–29

▼

KEY VERSES:
See that what you have heard from the beginning remains in you. If it does, you also will remain in the Son and in the Father. And this is what he promised us—even eternal life (1 John 2:24–25).

TODAY'S FOCUS:
Not everyone who claims to be a Christian really is one. Wisdom and discernment are needed to separate the true followers from those who would lead believers astray.

READ:
Pray for wisdom to discern who are true believers.

A. Some people will talk about religion, but will not truly be born of God. What are the characteristics of a genuine Christian?

Knowledge of Jesus' teaching +
Practice of those teachings.
Sharing with others - teaching
them to learn of Jesus on their
own, as well as from others
examples.

B. What are the characteristics of those who are not really true believers?

Speaking ō knowledge, professing
belief but not being able to
give an answer why.
lives don't match up ē Jesus' teaching
in every way.

C. Here is what I believe about Jesus Christ:

Son of God, died for my sin
on a cross, raised to life on
the third day, now sits on
the throne for judgement day.

NEED:

Pray for confidence regarding His coming.

My greatest need today is:

The Son met my need today _____ (date) in this manner:

DEED:

Pray for faithfulness to do what is right.

I desire to help others remain in Christ and avoid deceivers. Here's what I will do to accomplish this:

▲

APPLICATION:

People who are not true Christians are described in 1 Timothy 4:1–5 and 2 Thessalonians 2:1–12. How should you relate to such people?

TO LOVE LIKE GOD

1 John 4:1–21

▼

KEY VERSES:
This is love: not that we loved God, but that he loved us and sent his Son as an atoning sacrifice for our sins. Dear friends, since God so loved us, we also ought to love one another (1 John 4:10–11).

TODAY'S FOCUS:
God is the source and example of love. If you follow Him, you are to love as He loves—unconditionally, sacrificially, wholeheartedly.

READ:
Pray to love without being fearful.

A. We can tell others that people born of God
will experience the beauty of God's great
love. Why can we say this with confidence?

*As we follow God we love others
and others will feel Gods love
completely through us.*

B. People who are not from God will believe
false ideas. Describe what these people are
like. *Own judgement of where the
line between right + wrong is —
line moves according to their
lives — what they once held to as
wrong may now be acceptable.*

C. I will show God lives in me by:

*loving more fully all those
I encounter — from my
heart.*

DAY 24

NEED:
Pray for love for other people.
My greatest need today is:

The loving Father today _____ (date) answered my prayers by:

DEED:
Pray that people will listen to you.
Dear God, perfect Your love in me for I desire to share that love with:

▲

APPLICATION:
Do you want to know and experience God's great love? Read 1 Corinthians 13 to discover the characteristics of His love. Ask God to teach you to love with those qualities.

THE CHOICE THAT SEPARATES

Luke 16:13–31

▼

KEY VERSE:
He said to them, "You are the ones who justify
yourselves in the eyes of men, but God knows
your hearts. What is highly valued among men
is detestable in God's sight" (Luke 16:15).

TODAY'S FOCUS:
Salvation requires a choice—a choice to accept
God's gift and to live a life that is highly valued
in His eyes, not the eyes of men.

READ:
Thank God He knows our hearts.

A. Christ told this parable so that materialistic
people like the Pharisees, a religious sect
interested only in a superficial lifestyle,
could see God's truth. How does God evalu-
ate people? Their heart is read —
how do they do with what
was given them?

B. What are some characteristics of hell? Of
heaven (Abraham's side)?

Hot, tormented

Cool, refreshing, peaceful

C. I choose to serve God because:

He has given me life + I
long to be with him.

NEED:

Pray for your loved ones to trust Christ.
My greatest need today is:

The God of heaven answered me on _____
(date) in this way:

DEED:

Pray that lovers of money will become lovers of
Christ.
Dear Lord, I pray You will:

▲

APPLICATION:

Jesus told another parable about the kingdom
of heaven in Matthew 25:31–46. Will you be on
His right or left?

PUTTING YOUR FAITH ON THE LINE

Jude, verses 1–25

▼

KEY VERSE:
Dear friends, although I was very eager to write to you about the salvation we share, I felt I had to write and urge you to contend for the faith that was once for all entrusted to the saints (Jude, verse 3).

TODAY'S FOCUS:
Followers of Christ will have their faith put to the test. Only a most holy faith, a faith built up with prayer in the Holy Spirit, will endure.

READ:
Thank God He can keep you from falling.

DAY 26

A. God gives severe warnings to those people who deny Christ and live ungodly lifestyles. Describe what they are like and what will happen to them.

> Selfishly ambitious, out for their own gain, they will have eternal unrest.

B. What should God's beloved people do? What will Christ do for them?

> love one another, hold firm to the faith and Jesus will keep them safe until they are c̄ God —

C. I want my life to be characterized by:

> Mercy, Gentleness, Love Patience.

NEED:

Pray that you will keep yourself in God's love.
My greatest need today is:

The Holy Spirit helped me today _____
(date) by:

DEED:

Pray for determination to contend earnestly for
the faith.
O God our Savior, I pray You will use me to
snatch some people out of the eternal fire.
Lead me to:

▲

APPLICATION:

Do you have difficulty witnessing? List the reasons and what you will do to overcome them.

LIVE IN THE LIGHT OF THE FUTURE

2 Peter 3:1–18

▼

KEY VERSES:
Since everything will be destroyed in this way,
what kind of people ought you to be? You ought
to live holy and godly lives as you look forward
to the day of God and speed its coming (2 Peter
3:11–12).

TODAY'S FOCUS:
Someday this present world will be over. God is
patient in bringing about this destruction, not
wanting anyone to perish. What a merciful God
we serve!

READ:
Pray to live a holy and godly life.

DAY 27

A. What is going to happen to the heavens and earth? To ungodly people?

To be burnt up & destroyed

B. What should godly people do between now and the destruction of the world?

Try to save as many as possible from the fire that is to come?

C. In response to this passage, I will:

DAY 27

NEED:

Thank God He is patient with us.

My greatest need today is:

My Lord and Savior Jesus Christ, thank You
for answering my request on _____ (date)
in this way:

DEED:

Pray for your non-Christian friends to come to
repentance.

Lord, You are patient and don't want anyone
to perish. Therefore, help me to:

▲

APPLICATION:

The coming of the "Day of the Lord" is portrayed
in many passages. Begin your study of this
critical event by reading the book of Joel and 1
Thessalonians 5.

WHEN HISTORY STOPS

Revelation 20:1–15

▼

KEY VERSE:
Blessed and holy are those who have part in the first resurrection. The second death has no power over them, but they will be priests of God and of Christ and will reign with him for a thousand years (Revelation 20:6).

TODAY'S FOCUS:
The end of the world is coming and it is in God's control. Those who follow Him will share in His plan. Those who don't face eternal damnation.

READ:
Pray for a strong testimony for Jesus.

A. Death is not the end. God has promised a special conclusion to history. What will Christ do? What will His faithful followers do?

B. What will happen to these?

Satan	Death	Hades	People Not in Book of Life

C. This is how I respond to this passage:

NEED:

Thank God for His ultimate victory over Satan.
My greatest need today is:

The Lord Jesus Christ kept His Word today
_____ (date) by answering my prayer in
this manner:

DEED:

Thank God you are in the Book of Life.
All-powerful God, I am Your servant. Guide
me to:

▲

APPLICATION:

Continue to read about our awesome God and
the end of history in Revelation 19–22.

REWARDS OF A FEW WEEKS

1 Thessalonians 2:1–20

▼

KEY VERSE:
We loved you so much that we were delighted to
share with you not only the gospel of God but
our lives as well, because you had become so
dear to us (1 Thessalonians 2:8).

TODAY'S FOCUS:
Imparting the Word of God is more than merely
telling the message. It is living the message. It
involves caring, hard work, boldness, love, commitment, pure motives, encouragement, comfort, urging, and suffering. Without a doubt, it
is all worth the effort.

READ:
Pray to share your life with others.

A. Paul spent only a few weeks in Thessalonica. Yet, in that short time, he had a lasting effect on the lives of the Thessalonians. How did he treat them?

B. How did these people respond to Paul and the gospel message?

The Thessalonians	The Jews

C. For the next few weeks, I will work hard to:

NEED:

Pray that you will please God.
 My greatest need today is:

 The Lord Jesus met my need on _____
 (date) by:

DEED:

Pray that your loved ones will live lives worthy
of God.
 Thank you God, that Your message changes
 people who believe. I pray You will:

▲

APPLICATION:

Find out what else Paul did in Thessalonica.
Read Acts 17:1–9; 1 Thessalonians 1:1–10, and
2 Thessalonians 3:1–15.

REWARDS OF THREE YEARS

Acts 20:17–38

▼

KEY VERSE:
However, I consider my life worth nothing to me, if only I may finish the race and complete the task the Lord Jesus has given me—the task of testifying to the gospel of God's grace (Acts 20:24).

TODAY'S FOCUS:
Invest your life in people and God's mighty work among them. Someone has said, "You haven't changed a thing until you have a changed a life." Become a life-changer.

READ:
Pray that you will complete the task God has given you.

A. Paul had a reunion with his friends from
   Ephesus, where he had lived for three years.
   What had he done for them?

B. What motivated Paul to do these things?

C. Three years from today, I would like to have
   accomplished the following:

NEED:

Pray for strength to proclaim the whole will of God.

My greatest need for today is:

God has shown His purpose by answering my prayers today _____ (date) in this way:

DEED:

Pray for boldness to testify solemnly of the gospel of the grace of God.

Lord Jesus, as I declare and teach Your Word, I pray that:

▲

APPLICATION:

Paul had a great impact for God in Ephesus. Learn what happened there by reading Acts 18:19–21, 19:1–41, 1 Corinthians 15:32, and the book of Ephesians.

RESISTING THE PRESSURE TO GIVE UP

Acts 26:1–29

▼

KEY VERSES:
I was not disobedient to the vision from heaven. First to those in Damascus, then to those in Jerusalem and in all Judea, and to the Gentiles also, I preached that they should repent and turn to God and prove their repentance by their deeds. That is why the Jews seized me in the temple courts and tried to kill me. But I have had God's help to this very day (Acts 26:19–22).

TODAY'S FOCUS:
Never, never, never give up! Living for God and proclaiming His life-changing message will be challenged—by people and circumstances. Never, never, never give up.

READ:
Pray for courage to stand for Christ.

A. Imprisoned two years in Caesarea, Paul finally had a legal hearing before his accusers who had lied about him. How had Christ changed his life? What had Christ told him to do?

B. What message did he proclaim to all people?

C. Because of what Christ has done for me, I will testify:

NEED:
Pray for a changed life.
My greatest need today is:

Today _____ (date) Jesus of Nazareth has done this for me:

DEED:
Pray for enthusiasm to testify to both small and great.
O risen Christ, give me the opportunity to:

▲

APPLICATION:
What would cause you to give up? Write down your potential weak spots and ask God for His strength to conquer them. Move forward with His help.

KNOWING HOW TO WITNESS

Imagine you've just come upon an auto accident on a lonely stretch of road. As you run to a victim lying on the grass you realize that help is a long way off and you are untrained in emergency care. It seems to you that, though conscious, the person has but a few minutes to live. What would you tell him? How would you explain the gospel to this dying man in the two or three minutes left to his life? What would you say to anyone who needs to know God personally?

Over the past 31 days you have become more acquainted with God's heart for people. He wants people to experience His salvation, forgiveness, and presence for eternity. And He wants to involve you in the process of telling people about His love for them. Now, how do you put all of this into practice? Let's begin with the content of our message.

1. What is the gospel?

The gospel is multifaceted. Numerous word pictures are used by the biblical authors, too numerous to recount each in detail here. However, we will look at the highlights.

The apostle Paul summarizes the gospel in one of his letters to the Corinthians, saying simply that "Christ died for our sins . . . [and] that he was raised" from the dead (1 Corinthians 15:3–4).

The essential thing God wants everyone to know about is the death and resurrection of Jesus Christ. But Paul does not here explain why Christ had to die, what His death accomplished, or how we can benefit from it. We need to look elsewhere in the New Testament for the full significance.

   A. *Why Jesus died.* Jesus gave His life because we are incapable of earning God's acceptance. In fact, we are all subject to God's wrath because of our sin (Romans 1:18). Every one of us has sinned (Romans 3:9). When we compare ourselves with other people, it may seem that we are not so bad, but when our hearts are compared with God's righteousness, we fall short (Romans 3:23). And that is bad news because of the penalty for our sin—death (Romans 6:23).

Our sin created a barrier between us and God. Regardless of how much good we have done (and it may indeed have been quite extraordinary), we are not perfect. Thus, we are separated from God. Now this creates all sorts of other problems: alienation from ourselves, from other people, and from our environment. Our basic problem, though, is our alienation from God—and we are helpless to do anything about it.

B. *What Christ's death accomplished.* The night just before Jesus died, He established the Lord's Supper. When He offered the cup of wine to His disciples, Jesus said, "Drink from it, all of you. This is my blood of the covenant, which is poured out for many for the forgiveness of sins" (Matthew 26:27–28).

Christ changed our desperate situation: "We have redemption through his blood, the forgiveness of sins" (Ephesians 1:7). "He forgave us all our sins, having canceled the written code . . . he took it away, nailing it to the cross" (Colossians 2:13–14). His death accomplished the forgiveness of all our sins.

The punishment we deserved, eternal damnation, Christ took on Himself. As a result, the way is open for us to come to God. As Peter put it, "For Christ died for sins once for all, the righteous for the unrighteous, to bring you to God" (1 Peter 3:18). His anger is satisfied (1 John 2:2); our sins no longer require our separation from His presence. We are forgiven!

C. *How it can affect us personally.* In order to benefit from His death in our behalf and to experience His forgiveness, all we have to do is accept His forgiveness by faith. Paul writes, "For it is by grace you have been saved, through faith—and this not from yourselves, it is the gift of God—not by works" (Ephesians 2:8–9).

We may be tempted in some way to try to earn or work for His forgiveness, but that will not succeed. Forgiveness is offered freely as a gift. If you could do something to earn it, it would be a deserved wage, not a gift. We are saved by faith alone in Jesus Christ (Galatians 2:16–21, Titus 3:5).

Place yourself in this hypothetical situation: You've just died, and you're standing before God at the gates of heaven. The Lord asks you, "What have you done to deserve to be in My heaven?" How would you answer?

Many of whom I've asked this question respond with one of two answers: (1) "I did the best I could with what I had"; or (2) "I tried not to hurt anyone along the way." Yet, the only answer that will suffice is one along these lines: "I've done nothing to deserve to be in heaven. In fact, I deserve to be sent to hell forever. But I have trusted in Christ's forgiveness of my sins achieved for me by His death in my place on the cross." Only on this basis would God open the gates and gladly usher you into His eternal glory.

Let's return to the person dying along the side of the road. What would you say now? He does not need to hear nice stories or a list of regulations. He needs to know how to deal with his sin and receive eternal life, doesn't he?

2. How to get started

When you have a desire to witness, one of the biggest hurdles to get over is the beginning. What do you do first? Here are some practical instructions, most of them based on Colossians 4:2–6:

A. *List*—Make a list of people to whom you would like to explain the gospel.

B. *Pray*—Pray for open doors to share the joy of God's love with these people. Trust God for His guidance and power.

C. *Look*—Be alert to when those doors open and take the initiative to talk about Christ. Even if there's only a crack, see if it will open further.

D. *Prepare*—Review the essentials of the gospel and learn a simple outline for presenting its truth.

E. *Explain*—Learn to listen to people in order to know how to respond to them wisely and with graciousness, without watering down the content of the gospel.

If you diligently do these things, I assure

you that you will have many exciting opportunities to share God's heart for people.

3. How to handle your concerns

As you begin and continue to communicate the gospel to other people, you may have some concerns about the whole idea. Let's look at some of the most common issues.

A. "I'm afraid I won't know the answers to their questions." You may be asked to defend your belief in Christ. Some people will express objections or ask you questions. Study resource materials to learn some of the answers. *Answers to Tough Questions,* by Josh McDowell and Don Stewart, will be of great help. You may even find answers to some of your own questions.

Remember that it is okay to say, "I don't know; but I'll try to find out." Don't try to win an argument by getting upset. Explain with a loving attitude the reasonableness of the gospel. Simply help a person think his (or her) way to Christ and His forgiveness.

B. "I get off the track too easily and talk about other topics." Use a simple outline of the plan of salvation will help. You may want to purchase the booklet "Would You Like to Know God Personally?" by Dr. Bill Bright.

This concise booklet presents the gospel simply and logically. Read through it with someone, or ask him or her to read it. Then talk about its content. If the conversation wanders, you can always say, "It seems we're getting off-track—let's keep going on the main points of the booklet."

C. "I don't want to seem like I'm preaching." The gospel indeed has a personal impact in our lives, but it is not just a matter of personal opinion. There is a content to the gospel that must be believed in order for one to experience God's forgiveness and eternal life. So we relate that content to people, but in a loving manner.

If you feel like you're preaching to people, listen to your voice. You actually may have a preachy, judgmental attitude. Calm down. Communicate the gospel in a conversational tone. Allow the other person to talk and ask questions. Acknowledge his good points, and ask him questions. Your goal is to help him understand the gospel message and believe it.

D. "It seems so awkward, this talking about religion." In America, religion is private and often thought of as unrelated to any other parts of life. So when you bring up spiritual things, people sometimes bristle. You can overcome this reluctance by showing them how the gospel is connected to everyday affairs.

For example, a neighbor is talking about his resentment against his wife for something she's done. You can see if there is an open door by asking him, "Do you want to forgive her? What will happen to you and your marriage if you don't? Do you have the ability to forgive? Do you feel forgiven yourself? I know this is personal, but do you know what it's like to experience God's forgiveness?"

E. "Most people seem to be Christians already. They go to church and are basically good people." You know by now that the central issue is not a good life, but faith in Christ's death in our behalf to provide forgiveness of our sins.

4. Where to get training in evangelism

I encourage you to learn more about effective methods of leading someone to believe in Christ. Ask your pastor if your church or denomination has an evangelism training program which you may attend. There are several good interdenominational organizations that present excellent courses and publish materials to help you communicate your faith effectively.

A book I highly recommend is *Witnessing Without Fear* by Bill Bright. If you've ever been reluctant to witness, I encourage you to read this book. Sharing from more than thirty years of personal experience, Bill Bright illustrates how to overcome the two obstacles which prevent most Christians from telling others about Christ: fear and lack of know-how.

For an in-depth study of evangelism, which includes the philosophies as well as the practicalities of witnessing, no book is better than *Tell It Often—Tell It Well*. Mark McCloskey writes, "Our evangelism must reflect a warm heart and a trained mind so that as many as possible might listen, and that those who listen may truly hear." You'll be encouraged to share the good news more often and to develop your own specific plans for reaching out to others.

IMPORTANT WORDS TO UNDERSTAND

Adoption—being included in God's family. Every person is a creation of God, but only those who have been included in His family by faith in Christ's death are children of God. **Romans 8:14–15.**

Circumcision—Jewish rite in the cutting off of the foreskin of a newborn male as a sign that he is a Jew. In the New Testament it can sometimes symbolize a heart commitment to the Lord. "Uncircumcision" refers to non-Jews or to those who, under the Old Covenant, do not belong to God. **Colossians 2:11–12.**

Eternal Life—knowing God intimately forever; the best of living. For all who have placed their trust in Christ, it is a satisfying, present possession and an infinitely greater reality after physical death. **John 17:3.**

Grace—God's undeserved favor. It is especially seen in His love and kindness toward us. **Ephesians 2:4–5.**

Justification—being declared righteous by God. It is a legal statement saying that we've done everything right and nothing wrong. **1 Corinthians 6:11.**

Mercy—Compassion toward others. In reference to God, it is His favorable attitude and actions toward sinful, undeserving people. **1 Peter 1:3–5.**

Propitiation—God's anger is satisfied. Due to our sin, God was angry with us, but this anger was taken care of by Jesus' death in our place. **1 John 4:10.**

Reconciliation—being brought back to God. When we sinned, we removed ourselves from God. Sin formed a barrier between God and us, but He has removed that barrier, allowing us to be brought back to Himself. **2 Corinthians 5:17–21.**

Redemption—being purchased from oppression.

We were oppressed by sin and were under judgment, but God brought us back (ransomed us) through the death of Christ. **Ephesians 1:7.**

Renewal/Regeneration—beginning of our new life in Christ. When one trusts in Christ's forgiveness, God places His Holy Spirit in that person, and the Spirit makes God's life real in his life. **1 Peter 1:23.**

Salvation—Deliverance from sin and evil. Only God can accomplish this. Through the death and resurrection of Jesus Christ He has offered deliverance to all who put their faith and trust in Him. It covers three main areas: (1) Past—from the penalty of sin; (2) Present—from the power of sin, and (3) Future—from the presence of sin. **Hebrews 9:27–28.**

Sanctification—being made like God. God asks us to join with Him (via His empowering) in the lifelong process of becoming like Him. **1 Corinthians 1:2.**

Sin—any and all falling short of God's glory. It is both (1) a governing principle within us which rebels against God's will (as revealed in His Word); and (2) any act which fails to reflect His glory. **Romans 3:23.**

Successful witnessing—simply taking the initiative to share the gospel of Christ in the power of the Holy Spirit and leaving the results with God.

Wrath of God—God's just and fierce anger at sin and those who persist in it. God is a righteous judge and will destroy those who do not meet the standard of righteousness. His wrath is satisfied by Christ's death. **Revelation 19:15.**

ADDITIONAL
31-DAY
EXPERIMENTS

Now that you have finished a month of studying God's Word and growing closer to God, I hope you will want to continue to spend time alone with the risen Lord. He is the Vine from whom you can receive daily life and nourishment. Intimacy with Him continues and increases as you daily remain in Him.

The *31-Day Experiment* series of books has been designed to help you develop a consistent devotional time with your Heavenly Father. Whether you are a new Christian or have been one for a long time, these *31-Day Experiments* will help you establish an intimate relationship with Christ. You will experience for yourself the joy of discovering God's truth from the Bible.

Although all the Experiment books are designed like the one you have just completed, each book includes different passages and themes for you to study.

At the end of each Experiment is a number of simple Bible study methods or ideas for further growth. These will help you investigate, on your own, more of the truth that the Holy Spirit has given for you to know.

These books are designed to help you get into God's Word, and get God's Word into you:

GROWING CLOSER TO GOD

This is the original *31-Day Experiment* book. It is designed to help you cultivate your knowledge of God by looking at passages in which you can discover more about His ways and perspectives. The process of continuing to know God intimately will affect every area of your life and actually will begin to transform you into the kind of person He wants you to be.

Some of the topics included in the book are:
- God's Plan to Provide for My Needs
- Turning Pain Into Hope
- New Life and New Purpose
- Guidelines for Spiritual and Physical Health
- The Truth About Temptation
- Path to Personal Peace
- The Pleasure of Pleasing God

Two additional simple Bible study methods at the back of the book are explained for you to try. The **first** is a "One-a-Week Bible Topics." You will learn how to find out all that God says on any biblical subject that interests you.

The **second** is "15 Characters for 15 Days." You will be able to investigate the lives of biblical people. To start you off, 15 people are suggested. They each can be studied within only 30-45 minutes. The Holy Spirit can teach you some vital lessons through these and other biblical characters.

A PERSONAL EXPERIMENT IN FAITH-BUILDING

God wants your faith to grow. This Experiment book is a biblical study to build your faith in the manner that Christ desires. What ingredients are needed to develop a powerful trust in the Living God? They involve three areas: *knowledge, affirmation*, and *reliance*. You will learn how to increase all of them.

For 16 days you will learn how the Lord Jesus Christ developed the faith of His disciples. Both their successes and failures can teach you to believe the Son of God for greater things in your own life. The rest of the month will be spent observing what the apostle Paul says about building a biblical faith that can unlock for you the supernatural power of Almighty God.

You will learn how to feast upon God's everlasting Word by learning to study "The Great Moments of Faith." Throughout the Bible there are critical events that have shaped the course of history. Who were the people who trusted the Lord against unbelievable odds? Find out how to discover the secrets of their confident faith.

STANDING STRONG IN A GODLESS CULTURE

"Godless" is the word that best characterizes our culture today. People live as though the Lord does not exist. Their days are filled with things to do, and the thought of God seldom enters their minds. Christ is irrelevant to their behavior, decisions, lifestyle, and thoughts.

However, the people who know God will be strong and take action. They will shine as lights in this darkened world. God is not looking for superhuman people. He is looking for ordinary people who love Him and will trust His supernatural power.

This Experiment book will prepare you to become strong in the powerful might of the King of Kings. Here are some of the topics you will study during the 31 days of conquering obstacles:

- God Fights for His People
- The Consequences of Obedience
- To Slay a Giant
- Experiencing the Power of God's Word
- Resisting the Pressure to Conform
- The Sustaining Presence of Christ

You also will learn how to do a "Whole Book Study." To study an entire book of the Bible is to capture the heartbeat and powerful message of the divine Author.

Imagine being able to put the entire outline of a biblical book on one sheet of paper. You will start with Jonah. After that, you are encouraged to do a book chart of any other book of the Bible. Finally, there are practical suggestions for using your biblical knowledge to help others build a godly foundation for their lives.

KNOWING GOD BY HIS NAMES

This book took me 13 years to write. I first became interested in the fascinating variety of the names of God when I was a pastor in Indiana.

I started a search in the Bible for God's names. A name to the people in biblical times meant something entirely different from what it does to us today. In our culture a name is given to a child to identify him/her from other people.

But a name in the Bible refers to a particular trait or characteristic about the person. If you understand the meaning of his/her name, you will know something very important about him/her.

Our great Lord has over 200 names! God has so many names because each one puts the spotlight on a particular aspect of His incredibly complex character. No one name could tell you everything there is to know about Him.

This Experiment gives you a different name to study each day. By learning about each name, your understanding of God will increase and your love for our wonderful Lord will grow deeper.

Here are some of the names you will study during the 31 days:

Father
God Almighty
Prince of Peace
LORD (Jehovah)
Most High God

Living God
LORD Who Heals
Son of Man
High Priest
King of Kings
Shepherd

Your prayer life will be transformed. When you have a specific need, you will be able to address God using the name which deals with that situation.

- Anxious? Lean on the Prince of Peace.
- Hurt? Experience comfort from the Heavenly Father.
- Guilty? Find forgiveness from the Lamb of God.
- Insecure and fearful? Look to the Rock.
- Looking for direction? Follow the Shepherd.
- Confused? Come to the Light of the World.

In the back of the book, you will find a list of all the names for God, their characteristics, and a key verse to get you started in learning about each name. In addition, there are practical directions to help you unlock the mysteries of God's divine person.

It is an exciting approach to developing a deep intimacy with the Lord of Glory. He wants to reveal Himself to you so that you will respond in obedience, faith, love, and worship.

BUILDING A POSITIVE SELF-IMAGE

Regardless of who you are or what you do, this Experiment book will help you put your life into a sharper perspective and give you insights into the person God wants you to be.

What do you think about yourself? Are you maximizing your spiritual gifts? Are you using your time wisely?

As you work through the book, you will spend 13 days studying passages in which God says significant things about how to look at yourself. Your confidence in understanding who you are in God's eyes will increase. Then for 18 days you will study passages that will help you live life to the fullest. You will learn practical things you can do to make your life count.

This fascinating experiment will help you overcome personal doubts and weaknesses. Clearly and powerfully it helps you see the real truth about yourself from God's perspective. You will learn specific suggestions for living your life to the fullest with significance. Your relationship with the Lord who created you will be enhanced as you spend daily time with Him.

Here are some topics you will study to help you develop a biblical self-image.

- What does God say about you?
- Learning to invest your life wisely.
- How to improve yourself.
- Discover and develop your spiritual gifts.
- How to conquer doubts.
- Learn to be truly happy.
- What does it mean to "renew your mind"?
- Love like God loves.
- Rejoicing in difficulties.
- Build a precious heritage.
- Focusing on your ultimate future.

These and other important topics will give you a positive perspective on yourself and your life.

ABOUT THE AUTHOR

Dick Purnell is the founder and director of Single Life Resources, a ministry of Campus Crusade for Christ. He is an internationally known speaker and author.

A graduate of Wheaton College, Dick holds a Master of Divinity degree from Trinity Evangelical Divinity School and a master's degree in education (specializing in counseling) from Indiana University.

Dick has authored eight books in the *31-Day Experiment* series. He has also written *Friendship . . . The Basis for Love, Building a Relationship That Lasts* and *Free to Love Again.*

He and his wife Paula have two daughters, and they live in North Carolina.